I0762661

Little Mitchie

MONSTER MUNCHIES

SPOOKY SNACKS ALL YEAR LONG

KIDS IN THE KITCHEN

Joanne Mattern

CREATING YOUNG NONFICTION READERS

Little Mitchie books spark curiosity and support early nonfiction reading for students in Grades 2-3. Designed to build vocabulary, support second language learners, and prepare readers for middle-grade content, each book includes helpful tips for parents and educators to build confidence and deepen understanding of the world.

TIPS FOR READING NONFICTION WITH BEGINNING READERS

Talk about Nonfiction

Begin by explaining that nonfiction books give us information that is true. The book will be organized around a specific topic or idea, and we may learn new facts through reading.

Look at the Parts

Most nonfiction books have helpful features. Our *Little Mitchie* titles include color photographs and graphic aids, a table of contents, a glossary, and an index. Share the purpose of these features with your reader.

Color Photos and Graphic Aids

A lot of information can be found by "reading" photos, charts, maps, and other graphic aids found within nonfiction texts. Help your reader learn more about the different ways information can be displayed.

Table of Contents

Located at the front of the book, this list shows the big ideas within the text and the page numbers where they can be found.

Glossary

Located at the back of the book, the glossary defines key words and phrases that are related to the topic. These words and phrases can be found in the text in colored type.

Index

Located at the back of the book, an index is an alphabetical list of topics and the page numbers where they can be found.

With a little help and guidance about reading nonfiction, you can feel good about introducing a young reader to the world of *Little Mitchie* nonfiction books.

Little Mitchie is an imprint of:

Mitchell Lane
PUBLISHERS

2001 SW 31st Avenue
Hallandale, FL 33009
mitchelllanepub.com

First Edition, 2027.

Author: Joanne Mattern
Designer: Bobbie Houser
Editor: Madison Greve

Library of Congress Cataloging-in-Publication Data
Title: Monster Munchies: Spooky Snacks All Year Long / by Joanne Mattern

Description: Hallandale, FL : Mitchell Lane Publishers, [2027]

Identifiers:
ISBN 979-8-89260-928-9 (library bound)
ISBN 979-8-90145-014-7 (eBook)

Library of Congress Control Number: 2026936535

PHOTO CREDITS
Alamy: GL Archive, 21; Shutterstock: GreenArt, cover, 1; Taras Grebinets, 4; Viktoriia Ablohina, 5; AmyLv, 7; The Image Party, 9; apolonia, 11; Ajm_a_l66, 13; JeniFoto, 15; KVMArt, 17; Elena Hramova, 19; Yalcin Sonat, 21.

TABLE OF CONTENTS

HOW TO USE THIS BOOK

The kitchen is a great place to have fun! This book will help you make some delicious recipes.

Read each recipe first. Be sure to have everything you need in place before you start. Check that no one is **allergic** to any of the ingredients.

Wash your hands before you start.

Have an adult close by. Let them use knives and the stove.

Now, get ready to cook up some fun!

CONVERSION CHART

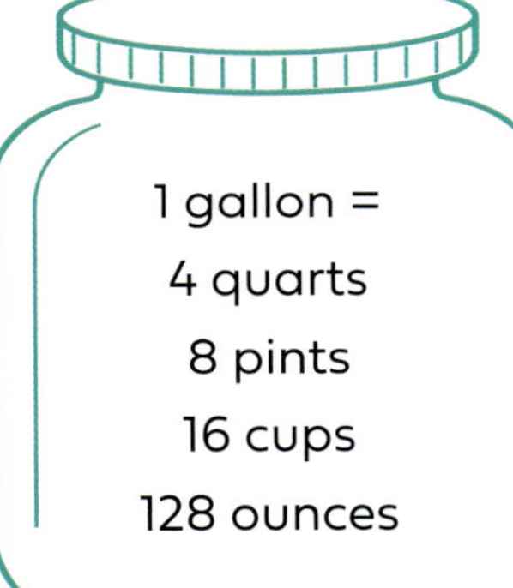

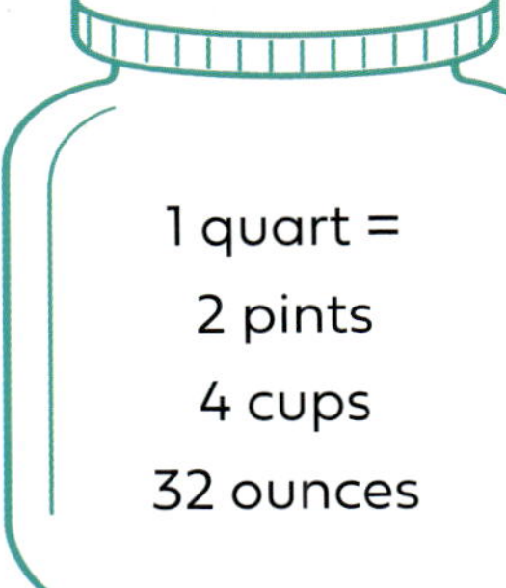

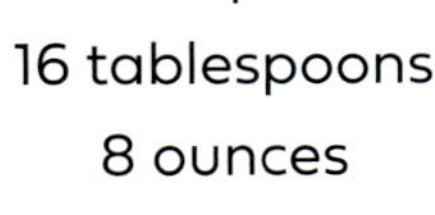

1 cup =
16 tablespoons
8 ounces

¾ cup =
12 tablespoons
6 ounces

½ cup =
8 tablespoons
4 ounces

⅓ cup =
5⅓ tablespoons
2⅔ ounces

¼ cup =
4 tablespoons
2 ounces

3 teaspoons = 1 tablespoon (½ ounce)
2 tablespoons = ⅛ cup (1 ounce)
4 tablespoons = ¼ cup (2 ounces)
5⅓ tablespoons = ⅓ cup (2⅔ ounces)
8 tablespoons = ½ cup (4 ounces)
12 tablespoons = ¾ cup (6 ounces)
32 tablespoons = 2 cups (16 ounces)

Chapter 1

WITCH HAT TREATS

"What do you want to bring to school for your class Halloween party?" Candace's father asked her.

"I saw a fun recipe online," Candace said. She pulled up the recipe on the computer.

"That looks easy enough to make," her father said. "Let's get started!"

Her father was right. The recipe was easy to make. It was fun to **decorate** the treats. "I can't wait to bring these to school!" Candace said when they finished. "Thanks for helping!"

You will need:

1 package of chocolate sandwich cookies

9-ounce bag of Hershey's Kisses™

1 tube of orange decorating frosting

1 container of Halloween sprinkles

Directions:

Place the cookies on a tray.

Add a circle of frosting to the top of 1 cookie so that it is almost covered with the frosting, but not quite.

Press a Hershey's Kiss™ into the frosting. This is your witch's hat!

Add some sprinkles around the frosting to decorate.

Repeat until all the cookies have a hat and sprinkles.

FUN FOOD FACT!
The Hershey Company™ makes more than 80 million chocolate Kisses every day!

Chapter 2

POPCORN FIT FOR A MONSTER

"Trick-or-treating was fun!" Joshua said as he and his sister came inside. He held up his bag. "We got lots of candy and other treats!"

"We walked for miles," his sister Elizabeth said. "I'm starving!"

"I thought you would be hungry," said Mom. "Remember the snack we made before you left? Now would be a great time to eat it."

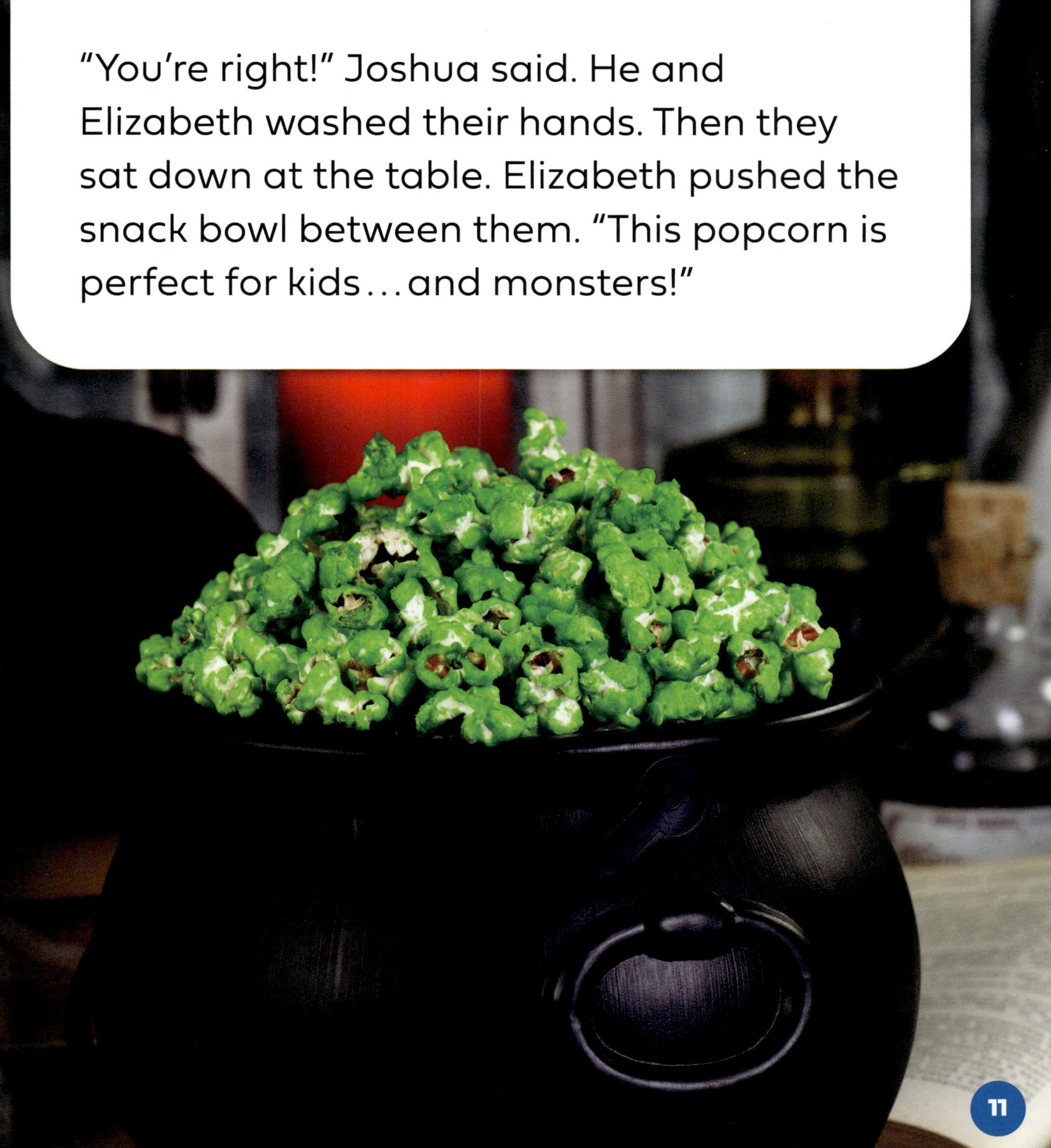

"You're right!" Joshua said. He and Elizabeth washed their hands. Then they sat down at the table. Elizabeth pushed the snack bowl between them. "This popcorn is perfect for kids . . . and monsters!"

You will need:

10 cups popped popcorn

½-cup brown sugar

¼-cup butter

16-ounce package of marshmallows

5 drops green food coloring

Directions:

Pour the popcorn into a large bowl.

Add the brown sugar and butter to a **saucepan**. Ask an adult to heat the mixture on the stove over medium heat. Stir until the butter melts and the sugar is mixed in.

Stir in the marshmallows until the mixture is smooth. Then stir in the food coloring.

With an adult's help, pour the mixture over the popcorn. Stir until all the popcorn is covered.

Chapter 3

MONSTER MOUTHS

"I heard Aunt Judy is having everyone over for a monster party," Claire's mother said. "What do you want to bring?"

"I just saw a scary monster cartoon," Claire said. "The monsters had big mouths and big teeth. Can we make a treat that looks like a monster mouth?"

“I think so,” Claire’s mother said. “This recipe will be fun and good to eat!”

You will need:

2 apples

½-cup mini marshmallows

½-cup peanut butter

Directions:

Ask an adult to **core** the 2 apples so there are 16 slices.

Spread peanut butter on 1 side of 8 apple slices and lay them on a plate with the peanut butter facing up.

Line each slice with mini marshmallows. Press them into the peanut butter so they stick up like teeth.

Spread peanut butter on 1 side of each of the other 8 apple slices.

Place the slices on top of the marshmallow teeth with the peanut butter facing down to make the monster mouths.

Chapter 4

MONSTER MAC 'N' CHEESE

"It's monster night at school," Tracy told her father. "Everyone is invited to see the monster artwork and stories we made. I can't wait to show you the poem I wrote!"

"That will be fun," Dad said. "We'll go over after dinner. I made some food to put us in the monster mood."

"Monster mac 'n' cheese?" Tracy's little brother asked. "That's amazing!"

"Scary and delicious," Dad said. "Eat up, my little monsters!"

You will need:

1 box of macaroni and cheese

¼-cup milk

4 tablespoons butter

1 jar of black olives

8-ounce bag of frozen broccoli

1 ball of mozzarella cheese

Directions:

Ask an adult to cook the macaroni and broccoli. Use the directions on the back of the box or bag.

Ask an adult to cut the broccoli into small bits and slice the cheese ball into thin slices.

Add the broccoli to the macaroni, stir together, and spread the mixture on a large plate.

Lay 2 cheese circles in the middle of the plate to make the eyes. Add 1 olive slice to each eye and place 1 just below them to make the nose.

Use 5–7 olives to **outline** the mouth. Add the rest of the olives to the top of the plate to make the monster's hair.

FUN FOOD FACT!

Thomas Jefferson had macaroni and cheese in France. He loved it so much, he brought the dish home to the United States.

GLOSSARY

algae (AL-jee)—Living things that grow in wet places, make oxygen, and are food for many animals

allergic (uh-LER-jik)—having a bad reaction to a food

core (KOR)—to take out the seeds and middle part of an apple

decorate (DEK-uh-rate)—to make something look nice by adding color or treats

outline (OWT-line)—to make the shape of something using just a line or lines

saucepan (SAWSS-pan)—a deep pan with a handle, which is used for cooking

FURTHER READING

Owen, Ruth. *Halloween Treats to Make and Bake.* Gareth Stevens, 2024.

Wood, Alix. *Freaky Food for Halloween.* Enslow Publishing, 2023.

ON THE INTERNET

"43 Easy No-Bake Halloween Recipes for a Spooky Fun Party." On My Kids Plate.com
https://onmykidsplate.com/no-bake-halloween-recipes/
This article has lots of ideas for different scary-themed foods.

"No-Bake Halloween Desserts & Treats." Cooking With Janica.com
https://cookingwithjanica.com/no-bake-halloween/
Check out this article for many different Halloween and monster foods for kids and parents to make together.

INDEX

ABOUT THE AUTHOR

Joanne Mattern loves snacking and eating fun food! She has written many nonfiction books for children, including cookbooks and books about holidays. Joanne lives in New York State with her family.